To

Karen, Ollie and Oscar,
and Pippin who popped in

Mister Storyfella

is a storyteller, songsta, poet and potato juggler. Born in St. Albans, Hertfordshire, UK, he attended the Muriel Green Nursery School.

Nowadays he's wound up slap bang in the middle of the wild and wacky West Country dwelling beneath circling buzzards and cackling ravens on the edge of Dartmoor.

Living in this land of myths and legend is a constant challenge. Crossing the river to get to the shops without being accosted by Cutty Dyer, the ogre who lives under the bridge can be a tricky business. Driving across the moor and not being molested by the Hairy Hands is a feat most people don't have to worry about in their daily lives.

Still, Mister Storyfella does manage to roam far and wide without mishap most days of the year.

For over forty years he's told tales, sung songs and spouted poetry at thousands of events and venues including schools, festivals, deep dark woods, haunted castles, No 10 Downing Street and Zaatari refugee camp in Jordan.

Globetrotting Mister Storyfella has plied his trade in Argentina, Canada, Germany, Indonesia, Jordan, Malaysia, Morocco, the Netherlands, Peru, the Philippines, Russia, South Korea, Thailand, Turkey and the U.S.

This travelling talesman, pedlar of poetry and thoroughly modern troubadour is equally happy to sit by a fire sharing a tale or two with you and your friends or perform on a stage for hundreds of eager ears.

Unicorn In The Playground will give you a flavour of what this fellow's all about. It's a selection of old and new material; some to be spoken, sung or shouted out loud; some to be read curled up in bed.

If you'd like to find out more about what Mister Storyfella is up to (or even better book him!) take a look at his website.

www.misterstoryfella.co.uk

Contents

Listen To The Story Or Else ... !

Beyond the seven seas
And behind the Glass Mountain,
There is a wooden house
With a dog yapping in the yard,
Chickens pecking in the dirt
And smoke wafting up the chimney.

In that house there is a little old lady
Sewing an ivory button onto a cambric shirt.

In the folds of her brown skirt
There is a white flea.

In the belly of this flea
There is a city.

On the edge of this city
There is a tree with ninety-nine branches
And ninety-nine vultures.

Beside the tree there is a steaming swamp
Swarming with crocodiles, snakes and leeches.
And if you don't pay attention
To what you are about to hear
Those crocodiles, snakes and leeches
Will slip into your bed tonight
And you might not wake up in the morning.

So,
Listen to the story,
Or else ... !

Colin The Chocolate Kid

Colin loved to eat chocolate. He loved brown chocolate, white chocolate and really, really dark chocolate. If there had been red chocolate, green chocolate, blue chocolate, pink chocolate, stripey chocolate or spotty chocolate he'd have loved that too.

He didn't care if it was Fair Trade or Rough Trade.

Colin loved chocolate bars, chocolate buttons, chocolate biscuits, chocolate cake, chocolate flakes and chocolate ice-cream. He liked it so much he'd eat it at every meal.

Coco pops with chocolate milk for breakfast. Chocolate crisps and chocolate yoghurt in his packed lunch box. Chocolate-chip cookies with chocolate milkshake for his home time snack. Chocolate spread on bread for tea. Hot chocolate with a chocolate flake as a night cap tucked up in bed.

But don't worry, it wasn't that he wouldn't eat anything else. Sometimes he'd gobble fried eggs with chocolate sauce, baked beans with melted chocolate, chips with chocolate, burgers with chocolate, pizza with chocolate, chicken and chocolate, oodles of noodles with chocolate. He'd even eat Brussels sprouts so long as they had chocolate melted on them.

But the truth was, he wouldn't eat anything unless it had chocolate sauce squeezed on it or chocolate sprinkled over it.

Luckily, his mother couldn't stand the stuff, which was good news for Colin as that meant there was all the more for him. Often she'd warn him that one day he'd turn into a Chocolate Kid. He'd reply that he didn't care if he did.

Now one night, after a double hot chocolate with three chocolate flakes, Colin tossed and turned in bed. He just couldn't get to sleep. Do you think he'd had too much chocolate? I think you might be right.

He started counting sheep jumping over a fence. And yes, you've guessed, the fence was made of chocolate and so were the sheep!

One, two, three, over they went. But then, Colin noticed that a chocolate gate was open and the chocolate sheep had run out of the chocolate field and were escaping down the chocolate lane.

Colin jumped over the chocolate fence and ran along the chocolate lane. A chocolate bird sang from a chocolate tree beneath a chocolate sun in a chocolate sky.

Chocolate cows ate chocolate grass and chocolate daisies swayed in a chocolate breeze. Suddenly, to his surprise, Colin was driving a chocolate car along a chocolate road leading to a chocolate town.

He stopped at a chocolate zebra crossing and watched a chocolate mother pushing a chocolate buggy carrying chocolate twins sucking on chocolate dummies.

Then he found himself arriving at a big chocolate building. A chocolate man wearing a chocolate uniform opened the chocolate door of the chocolate car and led him into the chocolate factory where lots of chocolate people were making tons and tons of ... popcorn? ... marshmallows? No, don't be silly, they were making chocolate of course!

Chocolate people were pulling chocolate levers and pushing chocolate buttons. Chocolate steam rose from chocolate cooking pots. He climbed some chocolate stairs and walked along a chocolate platform above a huge chocolate vat full of tongue-tantalizing, lip-smacking, mouth-drooling chocolate.

It was all too much for Colin. He couldn't help

himself. He climbed over the chocolate railings and then dived headfirst into the quagmire of soft, milky-brown chocolate.

He swallowed the warm liquid as he swam deeper and deeper. When he reached the bottom of the chocolate sea he lay on his back with his belly full. Colin was in chocolate heaven.

And then he woke up.

'What a wonderful dream,' he thought.

As Colin was getting out of bed he noticed a strand of dark brown hair on his pillow. This was curious as the colour of his hair was blond. He picked it up and it felt strange. Not soft and light as air, but hard and brittle, and then it broke. Snapped in two. That was odd. Even more curious was the smell. It smelled of ... chocolate?

Colin sniffed it, and then he licked it, and then he bit it, and yes it really was his favourite food. Yum yum. It went down a treat.

He licked his finger and thumb and they tasted of chocolate too! And then he noticed both of his hands were made of chocolate!

Yum yum. Breakfast in bed!

He bit off his thumbs and then ate his fingers one by one. He was about to gobble what was left of his right hand when he realised that his feet, his legs, his arms, his tummy, his head, his whole body was made of the most delicious food in the universe.

Just as his mother has warned him. He'd turned into a Chocolate Kid.

He looked at his left arm. He looked at his right. They were both equally appetising. Which one to chomp first?

But then something in his chocolate skull – perhaps his brain was only half chocolatised – made him realise that if he carried on like this there wouldn't be much of him left by lunchtime.

He called out, 'Mum, come quick, I think I'm going to eat myself!'

But there was no answer. His mother had just popped out to the shops.

He panicked, rushing down the stairs, out of the house and into the street.

On the corner by the newsagents he saw his two chums, Connor and Courtney. He called to them, 'Help me, I've turned into a Chocolate Kid. I can't resist it. Stop me, I think I'm going to eat myself.'

They came up to him, pulled off his ears and laughed, 'Not if we eat you first!'

'Ow!' squealed Colin, before shooting off down

the road pursued by his so-called friends.

A bird flew from a tree and pecked off his nose. A dog chased him and bit off Colin's left foot.

Wherever he went someone or something wanted a piece of him. Even the pavement seemed to relish the trail of chocolate Colin left behind him.

Soon a crowd of people including aunts and uncles, policemen and teachers, shopkeepers and traffic wardens, footballers, pop stars and children were chasing Colin through the streets, parks and shops of the town.

Anyone who loved chocolate joined the

chase. Even you would have joined in if you'd had the chance. But you weren't there, so bad luck!

Poor Colin, by the end of the day there wasn't that much of him left to eat. What did remain lay under a hedge out of the sun and hidden from his pursuers.

As night fell, what looked like a battered bowling ball rolled and bumped along the sidewalk. It turned into Colin's front garden, jumped through the cat flap and bounced up the stairs into Colin's bed.

At last, lying on his pillow, Colin felt safe.

Just then, Colin's mother came into the bedroom.

'Hello Colin, I thought I heard you come in. Oh dear, you have been in the wars haven't you? Don't say I didn't warn you something like this might happen if you carried on with your chocolate fixation. Never mind. We'll soon have you as right as rain again.'

She went downstairs and soon returned with a large steaming bowl of chocolate soup. She spooned some into Colin's mouth and both of his ears grew back. With each mouthful, parts of his body returned. Soon the bowl was empty and Colin was almost back to normal. But unfortunately,

when he lifted up his hands there were still some parts missing.

'Don't worry, Colin. I've put aside a secret supply of chocolate biscuits.

'I think I've got just the right sort to finish the job properly.'

When she returned this time, she did

indeed have the right kind of biscuits. Each time she popped a biscuit into his mouth, another little part of his body appeared.

And yes, of course, you've guessed correctly. The biscuits were not chocolate digestives or bourbons, they were chocolate fingers, but unluckily for Colin, there were only nine left (because he had previously discovered his mother's secret hidey-hole).

But even more unfortunately for Colin, tomorrow was Monday and it was the first day back at school after the summer holidays. And if that wasn't bad enough, Colin was still made of chocolate!

So how will Colin The Chocolate Kid fare tomorrow? Will he last until lunchtime or will he devise a strategy to cope with this curious condition? Why not send me your ideas for the next chapter of Colin The Chocolate Kid?

Contact me via my website
www.misterstoryfella.co.uk

Juggling Potatoes

When you're juggling potatoes
As everybody knows
It is very funny
If you drop them on your toes

But you won't make much money
And the crowd won't feel so chummy

If you fumble
they will mumble

If you bumble
They will grumble

There'll be a right old rough and tumble
If *potaters* hit spectators

And spuds bonk them on the nose!

Our Dad's Not Normal

Our dad's not normal,
He is so uncool.
Our dad's not normal,
He always plays the fool.

He thinks the world's a circus
And that he is a clown.
He likes to cause a rumpus
As he ambles round the town.
He will talk to anyone,
He mimics people 'cos it's fun.
He'll dance a tango with a nun,
He's fifty but he thinks he's young.

He goes to parents' evenings
And tells teachers they are fools.
They should kick the system
And not stick to the rules.
When we go on holiday
He plonks his deckchair in the sea.
He wears his hat all wonky
And he dances like a donkey.

Our dad's not normal,
He is so uncool.
Our dad's not normal,
He always plays the fool.
He is so embarrassing
We won't be seen dead with him.
Our dad's not normal
But Mum thinks he's adorable.

How our mum puts up with him
Is a mystery.
What they've got in common
It is hard to see.
She's warm milky custard,
He's as hot as mustard.
She does not get flustered,
He is maladjusted.

Our house is like a junk shop,
Full of bits of tat.
When she wants to chuck stuff out
He says, 'Don't get rid of that!'

His socks are very smelly.
He's got a hairy belly,
It wobbles like a jelly.
You should hear him yelly
At the telly ...

'Switch that XXXX Factor rubbish off!'

Our dad's not normal,
He is so uncool.

Our dad's not normal,
He always plays the fool.
He is so embarrassing
We won't be seen dead with him.
Our dad's not normal,
It's not something that's ignorable.

It's all right when you're little,
It's all right when you're young.
A parent who's a riddle,
Can be a lot of fun.
But when you're a teenager,
A sad mad middle-ager
Is not something that you savour,
It does your street cred not one favour.

Our dad's not normal,
Our mates think he's a screwball.
Our dad's not normal,
The clothes he wears are terrible.
Our dad's not normal,
His sense of humour's laughable.
Our dad's not normal,
He says he's a free radical.

He's a jester, he's a fool,
He's the Lord of Misrule.
One thing he's not is sensible,
He is plain nonsensical.

Our dad's not normal,
And if you think he's odd –
You should meet his brother,
Uncle Rod.

Rover

After Sunday lunch I thought I'd take a nap,
But my best mate Rover wasn't having that.
I was dog-tired, but he was hot-wired,
He'd not be pacified, his sparks had fired.
He'd licked his own ignition
And was spewing out emissions.
I'd rather have preferred a pleasant stroll,
But Rover was raring to rock'n'roll.

I dashed out of the house –
grabbed the steering wheel,
The neighbour scowled as the fan belt squealed.
Next door's mutt was a very cross breed,
But his stumpy little legs
Couldn't match our speed.
Over the road humps we jolted and bumped,
A roundabout the wrong way –
Three red lights jumped.
A hound after a hare, following the scent,
Rover on his rush hour, head down, hell-bent.

We flew over the flyover
And reached the motorway.
Swerved around the vehicles that were in our way.
Cameras were recording every motoring offence,
It was such a miracle we caused no accidents.
I was a dogsbody hurtling through the traffic,
Though I gripped the gear stick,
The car was in dogmatic.
A pretty pink mini zipped up the slip road,
Rover leering to the left,
She veered off and we followed.

Bumper sniffing, exhaust whiffing,

                        down the country lanes.

Slowing and then speeding up,

                        she played her taunting games.

Tailgaters we, and teaser she,

                        we three enjoyed the sport.

Sidling along sidewalks, flirting on the forecourts,

Canoodling in lay-bys, off-road in fields of corn,

Rover, happy as Larry, honking on his horn.

She led a merry dance, she drove us round the bend,

And that's where this car chase saga ends.

Rover crashed into an ash

                        and I went through the screen.

I watched myself hurled through the air

                        like in a dream.

The fuel tank punctured, petrol spraying up the tree,

A mangled metal machine canine doing a wee.

And then, like squirting mustard

                        and drowning a hot dog,

My faithful friend's engulfed in flame

                        in this sad travelogue.

Now I'm in the doghouse, no doubt I'll go to jail,

Rover'll roam no more – that's the end of this tale.

Eddie Sucked A Little Stone

Eddie sucked a little stone
He thought it was a sweet.
His brother gave it to him
As a special treat.

He rolled the pebble round and round
On his purple tongue.*
Then crunched and munched until his molars
Mashed it into gum.

He chomped and chewed and then he blew
A mountain of a bubble.
And when it popped his brother lay
Beneath a pile of rubble.

* He had just scoffed a packet of blackcurrant pastilles.

Keep A Poem In Your Pocket

Keep a poem in your pocket
Or a tale upon your tongue
Be sure that you have told it
Before the day is done

If you've a joke
Then do not choke it
A song has to be sung
If you've a word
Make sure you've spoke it
Play a fiddle
Bang a drum!

For it is never too late
If you can't whistle
You can hum
Don't get yourself into a state
It can be such fun

Participate
Don't hesitate
It will keep you young
Celebrate
What you create
Or else show us your bum!

Angry Dormouse

A field mouse lives in a field,
a wood mouse lives in a wood
but a dormouse does not live on a door.

I may be a *snore* mouse
I'm certainly a *gnaw* mouse
I am an omni*vore* mouse
And I am not *enor*-mouse.

I'm a protected by the *law* mouse
I'm the one that you a*dore* mouse
I think I'm a *phwoar* mouse
But I am **not** a Door Mouse!

I can be a *moor* mouse
Though I am not a *tor* mouse
Sometimes I'm a *floor* mouse
But I am not a *wall* rouse.
I'm a *roll up in a ball* mouse
But not a *sleeping in a drawer* mouse
And I don't live in *your* house
So I am **not** a Dooooooor Mouse!

Some think I'm like a *ghost* mouse
And though not a one to *boast* mouse
I'm a rare and rather *special* mouse
Not an *at your beck and call* mouse.
I don't want to be a *boor* mouse
But I'm a *rodent with a grouse* mouse
I'm a *can't take it any more* mouse!
I am **not** a Doooooooooooooooor Mouse!

Now I am a *sore* mouse
You've made me be a *roar* mouse
I'm a *sharpening my claw* mouse
I'm a *warned you once before* mouse.
This is a *definitely the last straw* mouse

You're making me a *war* mouse
I'll be a *shock and awe* mouse
I am **not** a Doooooooooooooooooooooooooooooooooooo
ooooooooooooooooooooooooooooooooooooooooooooooo
ooooooooooooooooooooooooooooooooooooooooooooooo
oooooooooooooooooo
ooooooooooooooooo
oooooooooooooooo
ooooooooo
oooooooo
oooooooo
oooooooo
ooooooooo
oooooooooo
ooooooooooooo
ooooooooooooooooo
oooooooooooooooooo
ooooooooooooooooooo
oooooooooooooooooo
oooooooooooooooooo
oooooooooooooooooo
ooooooooooooo
oooooooooooooo
oooooooooooor

Mouse!

Nice *is* Nasty

Nice is a nasty little word.

It should not be seen,

It should not be heard.

It should not be written,

It should not be said.

It should never ever get out of bed.

It should crawl away and say goodbye.

It should curl up in a ball and die.

Crow? No!

I don't want to be a crow ... No!
I don't want to be a crow ... No!
I'd rather be a mole and live in a hole.
I don't want to be a crow ... No!

Tomorrow, I take my flying test
And even if I try my best
I know I'll fail, and I will fall
Out of the sky, it's terrible.

Time and time again I've tried
To spread my wings and try to fly
But just as soon as I look down
Gravity pulls me to the ground.

I panic, I get in a tizzy,
My heartbeat stops and I feel dizzy.
You might just as well ask me to fly to Mars,
I close my eyes and I see stars.

I bump into a beech tree,
I crash into a fence.
I get tangled in the brambles,
It was an accident ...

That I was born a bird.
It's really quite absurd.
Rather than these frightful feathers,
I'd much prefer a coat of fur.

I don't want to be a crow ... No!
I don't want to be a crow ... No!
I'd rather be a mole and live in a hole.
I don't want to be a crow ... No!

Quacky Quacky Duck Duck

Quacky Quacky Duck Duck,
That's my name,
I am wild, I am not tame.
Quacky Quacky Duck Duck,
It's such a shame,
I can never go back to the lake again.

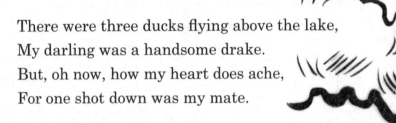

There were three ducks flying above the lake,
My darling was a handsome drake.
But, oh now, how my heart does ache,
For one shot down was my mate.

The hunter's gun went BANG! BANG! BANG!
One duck fell far from the land,
One duck fell by the waterside,
My love, he fell down by my side.

(And just before he died, he said ...)
'Quacky Quacky Duck Duck,
(as that's my name),
'Don't you become the hunter's game.
Quacky Quacky Duck Duck,
Don't be maimed,
Never come down to the lake again.'

These last words to me he said.
He kissed me once and then he was dead.
Then I heard the sound of the hunter's tread,
I shed my tears as off I fled.

Away, away from the water's edge,
That night I slept under a hedge.
And now I live in this old wood
And this is where I'll stay for good.

Quacky Quacky Duck Duck,
That's my name,
I am wild, I am not tame.
Quacky Quacky Duck Duck,
It's such a shame,
I can never go back to the lake again.

Buzzard Man

Call me a liar if you want to, though don't expect me to believe you, but there was once a poor farmer's wife who had a lazy old bag of bones for a husband. Every morning it was the same old story. While she was hustling and bustling around the farmyard, he'd be fast asleep in bed. His snores made the whole house shake until the pots and pans toppled out of the cupboards and the pictures fell off the walls.

The only way to wake him was to empty a bucket of water over his head. Then the wife would stuff

 him into his clothes and kick him down the stairs. It was all he could do to gobble down his porridge before he was shoved out of the door to tumble head over heels down the garden path. When he came to a stop, he'd look around at all the work needing to be done on the farm. He'd sigh and shrug his shoulders, lie down by the rhubarb patch and go to sleep until suppertime.

The cows were never milked or the eggs collected, the seeds were never sown or the crops harvested, unless it was by the poor old wife. The husband only lifted a finger to pick his nose or to scratch his bum. That is how it had been for years. But from today, things would be very different around the farm.

The day started very strangely indeed. The wife milked the chickens and collected the eggs from the cows. She was in such a tizzy that when she came into the house she pushed the husband out of the door with a sharper shove than ever. By the time he'd

tumbled to a stop he was so battered and bruised he couldn't lie down. It was then he looked up and saw a large buzzard circling above.

The husband shouted up to it,

'Lucky you, drifting about in the airy-fairy sky up there! You don't know what it's like to be a

h u m a n, tramping on the hard earth and having a scold for a wife. It's a simple life being a bird. All you do is flap your wings about a bit, then glide around taking it easy. You should come down here and find out what it's like to be a man who walks until his legs ache and works until his arms drop off.'

Well, with that, the buzzard swooped down and perched on the fence post next to him and said,

'All right, let's swap places.'

'How are we going to do that?'

asked the man, scratching his head.

'Easy,' said the buzzard, 'you give me your clothes and you can have my feathers.'

'What! Just like that?' said the man.

'Yes, just like that!' said the bird.

And so, the man became a buzzard and the buzzard became a man.

'How do I find my food?' asked the buzzard who had been a man.

'Oh, it's easy,' said the man who had been a buzzard. 'When you're up in the sky looking down from on high, you'll be able to see the scent of a dead creature rising from its carcass. Buzzards can see much better than humans. To their eyes, the smell rises like a kind of smoke.

'If it's a small creature, like a dead mouse, the smoke seems pink and wispy.'

'I don't like mice,' said the buzzard who had been a man.

'If it's a dead rabbit, the smoke is grey and light.'

'I don't mind rabbit,' he replied.

'If it's a dead deer, the smoke is black and strong.'

'I *do* like deer,' the other smiled.

The buzzard who had been a man flapped his wings and flew up into the sky and the man who had been a buzzard walked indoors to the wife.

He gave her a big hug and told the wife to sit down while he made her a cup of tea. Well, you can imagine, she nearly dropped dead with shock at that, and then she had to pick herself up off the floor after he told her he was going to be busy for the rest of the day.

He tidied up the farmyard and the vegetable garden, putting all the brambles and rubbish into a big heap. Then he called to the wife to show her all the work he had done. She watched as he struck a match and set fire to the pile. As the bonfire blazed a great spiral of black smoke rose up.

Suddenly, a buzzard swooped down through the smoke, plunged into the fire and was burnt to a cinder.

The wife gasped, 'Did you see that bird drop into the bonfire? What was it thinking of?'

'What a birdbrain,' said the man who had been a buzzard. 'You go indoors and put your feet up while I finish off here.'

A few weeks later, when the wife went to the market, a neighbour came up to her and said:

'What's got into your husband? Everybody's talking about him. He's changed.'

'What do you mean?' enquired the wife.

'Well, he's become hardworking and very polite to everyone nowadays it's true, but …'

'But what?' asked the wife.

'Haven't you noticed?' said her neighbour. 'When he thinks no-one's watching he starts rubbing his shoulders with his nose as if he's preening himself.

And what about those little feathers stuck to his clothes?

'And what about his nose? It's not the same one he had before. Now it's hooked and beaky. And he's got a strange smell to him. How can you put up with it?

'I was walking past your place the other day and I saw him trying to balance on a fence post. Last night, my Tom saw him up on your roof by the chimney pot making strange noises and flapping his arms about as if he was trying to fly!

'People are talking. They say he's not the man he was. He's acting like a bird. He's not a proper human. They say your husband is a Buzzard Man!'

'You hold your tongue,' said the wife. 'I'd rather have someone who works hard and cares for me than live with that lazy old bag of bones I had before. I don't care if he is a Buzzard Man. I like him just the way he is.'

And with that she stomped away to buy a couple of rabbits from the butcher's stall. She put them in her basket and made her way back home to prepare the supper.

That evening they sat at the kitchen table enjoying their meal. Her stew was delicious – rabbit braised in red wine with apricots and shallots. But her husband didn't like fussy food. He ate his meat red and raw, tearing it apart with his bare hands and washed down with a mug of dirty water.

And as far as I know, unless you can tell me otherwise, they both lived very happily ever after.

All Of The Cucumbers In The Glass Cloche

A branch from the oak
Breaks and plummets
Down to the vegetable bed.

Pip had just took off her bonnet
When the sky crashed down on her head.

Now all of the cucumbers
In the glass cloche
Lie battered and bloodied
Like her – sadly squashed.

Unicorn In The Playground

'Miss?'

'Who is that?'

'Miss?'

'Who is it?
Put your hand up!'

*'Miss?
Miss Thropple?'*

'Not again, Nancy,
I've explained all you need to know.
If you're short of ideas
Look to the whiteboard for inspiration,
For methods of punctuation
And examples of alliteration.'

'But, Miss?'

'What is it now?
Honestly, Nancy, aren't you aware

I've an objective to deliver?
Don't you understand?
You're not fitting in with the lesson plan.
We haven't got time to deviate,
Look at the time,
The lesson will come in late.'

'But, Miss, look through the window,
I thought that you should know.
There's a unicorn in the playground, Miss,
With a silver mane and horn,
On the tarmac galloping round and round.
Miss, are their young called foals or fauns?
I think it's looking for some grass, Miss.'

'Yes, Nancy, has it got a visitor's badge?'

'No, Miss, it didn't sign in.
I saw it jump over the high wire fence
Like a stone dropped into a pool.
What's it doing? It doesn't make sense,
Why has it come to our school?
It would have much more fun at my cousin's place,
There they have more time.

They don't feel they're in a race,
It's a better school than mine.'

'Nancy, turn around and look this way
And listen carefully.
There's an Ofsted inspector behind the door
With a list of things to inspect,
And a unicorn's not on it,
A horse with a horn on
Is not what he expects.'

'But there's a unicorn in the playground, Miss!'

'Don't be ridiculous, Nancy,
Unicorns do not exist!
Please do not persist.
And anyway,
We're not doing mythological creatures this term.
We're on a rolling programme,
They're not until the spring.
If it comes back then
We'll fit it in.'

'There's a unicorn in the playground, Miss,
It's acting very strange.

It's shaking its head and pawing the ground,
I think it's got the mange.'

'Nancy, stop it now!
You're leading the class astray.
Stop looking out of the window,
5A, face this way!

'Everybody pay attention!
You must complete this literacy lesson.
This creative writing exercise
Is running out of time.
You've only 13 minutes left,
Heads down now.
There's no need to rhyme.

'You're not to write a poem,
You're not to write a song,
And the whole piece needs to be
Exactly two sides long.'

'But the unicorn, Miss?'

'What is it now?'

'The unicorn, Miss,
 It's gone ...
I don't think it liked it here.'

'Good. Hopefully tomorrow
You'll get more work done.
You'll use your imagination in a more practical way.
In order to complete the task assigned,
I'll make sure there are no distractions.
Tomorrow, I'll pull down the blinds.'

'There was a unicorn in the playground, Miss,
There was, I swear it's true.
All the class were spellbound, Miss.
You poured scorn on a horse with a horn,
But the only one who couldn't see it ... was you.'

Why not draw your own picture of a unicorn in the frame?
(But not if this is a library book!)

Hamish The Hedgehurst

Once there was a creature
Who roamed upon this earth.
A curious strange mixture
From the day of its birth.
Half human and half hedgehog
The baby had been cursed.
His mother called him Hamish,
His father – the Hedgehurst.

His mother she did love him,
His father thought him weird.
His life, it was so grim,
Hamish Hedgehurst feared
That one day he'd be thrown
To the bottom of the well,
Strapped to a big stone
And nobody would tell.

So, on his cockerel he did ride,
Off he went to roam.
He no longer would reside
In the family home.

He travelled far,
He travelled wide,
Into the unknown,
And there he found the site to build ...

A Kingdom of His Own.

Where no-one would throw stones,
Where nobody would find him,
Call him names or break his bones.

A Kingdom of His Own.

A place where he could be himself,
A land where he was free.
A sanctuary to restore his health,
His own territory.

A
   Kingdom
      of
         His
            Own.

Blown Up By The Wind

Only just the other day
You wouldn't credit what befell me,
And I wouldn't blame you.
I hardly believe myself it's true.
I went out to do some shopping
To get some groceries for my tea.
The Meteorological Office had forecast rain
So I had dressed accordingly.
In my mackintosh and galoshes,
With my brolly and my trilby,
I was prepared for any splish-splash-sploshes
The elements might throw at me.

So, I was walking down the High Street
Pondering my future,
Wondering if I should settle down
Or embark on yet another adventure.
When all of a sudden, out of the blue
I was knocked out of my reveries.
Whoosh,whoosh,whoosh!
How the wind blew.
Then everything changed completely ...

It was gush hour in my home town,
There was panic on the street.
Debris flying all around,
It was all I could do to keep on two feet.
I clung to a lamp post,
A baby rolled by in a pram.
I reached out to grab it as it passed,
Next thing I know, there I am ...

Blown up by the wind, I was,
There was nothing I could do, of course.
Up in the sky in the blink of an eye,
I didn't have time to say goodbye.
I kept my umbrella but I lost my hat,
I was high as a kite in seconds flat.
I looked around, I was amazed,
I didn't dilly-dally, I was dizzy and dazed.

So there I am, up in the sky,
Bits and pieces pass me by.
My hat comes back
And hits me in the eye.
It's rather dangerous up this high.
Even the birds are too scared to fly.
Could the end be nigh?

Then I'm blown into the middle of next week
And still the wind is howling.
I find myself on a mountain peak,
The devastation is astounding.
I huddle in the middle of a flock of sheep,
Rocks are tumbling, trees are falling,
I'm in about ten fleeces deep –
My, how they bleat and how they reek,
I'm safe for a second but then I shriek.

Blown up by the wind, I was,
There was nothing I could do, of course.
Up in the sky in the blink of an eye
We didn't have time to say goodbye.
I'd lost my umbrella but I kept my hat,
We were high as a kite in seconds flat.
Looked around, I was amazed,
I didn't dilly-dally, I was dizzy and dazed.

Whipped up in a whirlwind,
Spinning like a top,
I wonder where we'll all end up.
I lost my bearings long ago,
Where we are now, heaven knows.
Then sudden as it had begun ... it stopped.

Uh-oh!
I must be up ten thousand feet.
The earth is looming nearer
At me and giant snowball sheep.
We're all in this together.
Just as I think we're all dead meat,
Who should come through the ether
But Little Bo Peep, who entreats,
'Here you are fella, here's your umbrella!'
God bless the shepherdess!

So, there I am with my makeshift parachute,
Drifting gently down.
Little Bo Peep had found her sheep
But then got splattered on the ground.
Buildings below look minute,
But soon I recognize some people.
They ask me where it is I've been
As I alight on the church steeple.

Blown up by the wind, I was.
There was nothing I could do, of course.
Up in the sky in the blink of an eye
I didn't have time to say goodbye.
I lost my umbrella but I got it back,

I was high as a kite in seconds flat.
Looked around, I was amazed,
I didn't dilly-dally, I was dizzy and dazed.

They didn't believe it,
So I had to repeat it ...

The Emperor's White Elephants

Once there was and twice there wasn't, an emperor in Asia who was a mean and miserly man. He would rather cut off his nose and eat it, than part with one more piece of his gold or silver. He'd become a hand-wringing, cheek-twitching, teeth-grinding kind of a tyrant.

It was all his grandfather's fault. When he had ruled, many moons ago, he'd heard of another emperor in the land next door who boasted of having the one and only white elephant in the world.

That very day his grandfather decreed that if any of his people could bring him a white elephant they would be handsomely rewarded with a lump of gold the size of the elephant's head.

Now, although you or I may not have seen a white elephant, that doesn't mean they don't exist. They are very shy and spend most of their time hiding in places you'd never dream of looking, but before long, the emperor's grandfather had so many white elephants he didn't know what to do with them all.

Those of you who have a pet or a zoo will know that looking after animals is a very expensive business. Not only did he have to feed and house them, he also had to give a big chunk of gold to every person who brought him one.

And remember, elephants, whether grey, yellow, red or white live for a very long time, and they have children too!

When the emperor's grandfather died, his son, the present emperor's father, had tried to stop this exorbitant custom. He'd also wondered about releasing the white elephants and letting them go back to where they'd come from, but his wise men advised him that once an emperor has made a decree it must stand for one hundred years.

There was still one year left to go and the current emperor had only one chunk of gold and nine thousand nine hundred and ninety-nine silver coins left in his coffers. In order to pay for the upkeep of the elephants he raised extra taxes from his people. He was sick of the sight and the sound and the smell of the costly creatures and had secretly ordered his tiger hunters to kill all the remaining white elephants in the wild.

As you can imagine, he wanted to hang on to his rapidly diminishing wealth and so had to make some drastic cutbacks.

Instead of three wise men, now he'd only two. Instead of two servants to help him dress, he'd only one and instead of one servant to brush his teeth, he'd learned to do it himself.

And the worst of it was he'd had to dispense with the Royal Storyteller. For if there was one thing he loved more than anything else in the world it was a good story. Especially one that took his mind off elephants!

But now he thought of nothing else. In the past, the silver-tongued Royal Storyteller had spun words that glittered and had woven tales that shot from the mouth like shooting stars that fell into his ears to make his heart fizz. Now his heart felt as flat as a cow pat.

He called for his two wise men who scurried like nervous weasels into the room as if they'd have their tails chopped off if they were a second late.

'I need a story a day
            to keep the elephants at bay.
A tale must be told but I will not pay.
I want one today, do not delay!
You're the wise men – what do you say?'

Well, the wise men, who weren't that wise at all but didn't want to lose their jobs, had to come up with something. And to find that something, they walked on hot coals, put ants in their pants and jointly wore the Ancient Necklace Of Crocodile Teeth while dancing a jig. But that something wasn't truly found until they hit each other ten times on the head with a hammer.

And that something was ... a Lying Competition.

'A Lying Competition?' said the emperor.

'$Y_Y^Y e_e^e E_s^S S_S$, a $L_L^L L Y_i^I N_n^g G$ $Co_o^o o_o^o o^O$mpetition.' replied the wobbly wise men.

'Explain yourselves!' shouted the emperor.

The wibbly wobbly wise men explained the best they could, which was very difficult since they were still suffering from the dizzying effects of a ten-pound bonk on the bonce.

But the upshot of it was, it would be announced that if anyone could tell the emperor a tantalising story of trickery and twists, if they could tell a terrifically tall tale that had never been told, one that took the emperor to the edge of his seat with disbelief, so that when the storyteller finished, the emperor declared the tale to be an utter load of porky pies, they would then receive the grand prize of a chunk of gold the size of an elephant's head for their wonderful wordy ways.

'What!' erupted the emperor. 'You idiots. I can't afford to pay the Royal Storyteller and I'm certainly not going to part with my last piece of gold!'

'But that's just it, Your Eminence, you don't. You let the storytellers have their say until, when they've finished, you tell them their tale wasn't a very tall tale after all, you believed every word of it and then you kick them out of the palace without even a silver coin for their trouble.

'All you have to do is remember not to call the storyteller a liar. That way you'll have a story every day and will never have to pay.'

'What a weaselly pair of wise men you truly are. Take the rest of the day off and put your heads in a bucket of ice.'

And for the rest of the year the emperor had a brand new story every day.

Wordslingers and Ear Ticklers came from far and wide with their fibs and whoppers and porky pies, with their cock and bull shenanigans and delicious deceits, lies and audio japes. But, however much the emperor enjoyed the tales, however much his eyes boggled with astonishment and his mouth *oohed* and *aahed* in wonder, however much he was drawn in like a fish to a worm on the end of a hook, at the final moment he remembered his last lump of gold and declared the story was perfectly possible, easily feasible and therefore as true as a turtle.

And so the finest storytellers in the land were sent off with fleas in their ears and went home downcast like dogs with their tails between their legs.

The emperor though, went to bed as happy as Larry for the next three hundred and sixty-four nights. Not only had he wonderful stories to send him off to sleep, but also, the day after tomorrow, he'd be free of the cost of looking after his white elephants. He had ordered their release. If his people thought white elephants were so wonderful *they* could look after them.

He still had his lump of gold the size of an elephant's head, his nine thousand nine hundred and ninety-nine silver coins and, if he didn't lower the taxes taken from his people, he'd be able to reinstate the Royal Storyteller and pay him to tell three stories a day.

Those weaselly wise men had certainly earned their weight in gold (but he wasn't going to give them that!), but as a reward he invited them to hear the tale of the last of the competitors for the Lying Competition.

And so, the next morning, all three waited eagerly for a tall tale of imagination and intrigue told by the

Blagger of Baghdad perhaps,
or even by the Chatterbox
of China, but they were
a little disappointed
when a grubby girl
wearing torn and
tatty clothes walked into the royal chamber holding
a bronze bell in one hand and with nothing on her
feet but mud.

But before they could complain or kick her out
she started her tale, which went like this ...

'Not that long ago, and yet it was the day
after tomorrow, I heard of an emperor who
loved stories. He wished to hear a very tall
tale. So I set off on my way and the tallest
thing I could see was a mountain. I put it
in my pocket but it fell out and smashed. I
pulled up a tree but it turned into a billion
birds that flew away. I picked up a tall tower
but it turned into a firework and we fizzed
off into space and exploded into a shower of
stars.

'When I fell to earth a few seconds later,
I heard a white elephant and a pink mouse

sobbing. I asked them what was wrong and they said they'd just returned from their honeymoon and found their nest had been swept away in a monsoon with all their possessions.

'I told them not to worry as I knew of a kind and generous man who loved nothing better than housing and feeding white elephants. Indeed, he would think it an honour to look after another one, especially as it was newly married to the prettiest, dinkiest, pinkiest mouse in the land.

'And besides, this man was an emperor who would give the couple his last nine thousand nine hundred and ninety-nine silver coins as compensation for the belongings washed away in the storm.

'Well, the elephant and the mouse were so excited at the thought of living in the grounds of a palace they said they wouldn't need the silver coins, but I could have them as a reward if I showed them the way.

'And so the elephant picked me up with his trunk, put me on his head and the little pink mouse carried us both to the palace.

'Indeed they're outside right now, resting in a tree. All I have to do is ring this bell and they'll come down.'

By now, as you can imagine, the emperor's face was as pale as the whitest elephant. The thought of giving away all of his silver coins to the grubby little girl was too much to bear. He whispered to his wise men.

'This story can't be true, can it? You can't put a mountain in a pocket, can you? Isn't it against the law for an elephant to marry a mouse?'

The wise men unrolled dusty scrolls and consulted with experts in this and that and eventually concluded that the tale just told was almost certainly, possibly definitely, a lie and should be declared as such.

With relief, the emperor announced his verdict.

'How dare you walk into my palace without washing your feet and then tell my wise men and I

a pack of lies
that swarmed like
flies around a pile of dung.
Be off with you girl and ring your
bell as much as you wish. For no elephant
or mouse will come down from that tree or
any other and I will not part with a single silver
coin. You should be ashamed of yourself. You are
a dirty rotten filthy liar and a discredit to your
mother and father.'

'Oh, I think my parents will be very proud of me,'
the girl retorted.

'And why is that?' the emperor and the wise men
laughed.

'Simply because I am cleverer than you and your wise men put together. You've called me a liar, so hand over the lump of gold!'

And with that the emperor realised he had indeed been tricked by someone much wiser than his advisers.

He picked up a ten-pound hammer and bashed ninety nine-inch nails into the heads of his worthless wise men who wobbled away like drunken porcupines. But before he gave the lump of gold to the grubby girl with the bell in her hand, he begged her to become his one and only wise girl so she could counsel him on how the white elephants could all live happily ever after. (Without him having to pay for it, of course.)

You might also be interested to learn she had some wizard ways of filling the emperor's coffers and that she was invited to replace the Royal Storyteller.

Whether she took up any of these offers, or did any of these deeds, is none of your business, as it's none of mine. And anyway, I've told you too much already, so now I'm going to stop before I get us all into trouble.

Where Did He Go?

Where did he go,
The boy who smiled?
Where did he go,
Who's now so wild?

Where is he now,
That thoughtful child?
Where is he now,
Once kind and mild?

Where did he go
When he ran out the gate?
Where did he go
When he came home late?

Why did he come back
In such a state?
Why did he come back
So full of hate?

Gone Missing

I looked in the mirror,
But nobody was there.

I peered in closer,
I couldn't see me anywhere.

I called out,
No-one said hello.

What's all this about?
I'd like to know.

'Come back please,
I don't want to be alone.

Don't be a tease.'
Then I called me on my phone.

I heard it ring
Inside the glass.

So I stepped right in,
'Who's this?' I asked.

Then I heard my voice
Inside my ear.

It said, 'Peek-a-boo!
I'm over here.'

I looked out of the mirror
And tried to get back.

But, to my horror,
I was caught in a trap.

I saw myself
On the other side,

An evil elf.
'Let me out!' I cried.

And ever since
I've been stuck inside.

Ever since
I've been ... stuck ... in ... side.

Stuck On His Face

He liked to dress up,
He liked playing games.
Changing his voice,
Changing his name.
But he'd always go too far,
He would never learn.
Now he's gone somewhere
From which he can't return.

Stuck on his face!
Stuck on his face!
He's got a mask
Stuck on his face!
He's not who he was,
An extraordinary case.
He's got a mask
Stuck on his face!

He went to a party
Disguised as someone else.
Got carried away,
Couldn't help himself.
Upset a lot of people,
Brought the party to an end.

'It was just a joke,' he said.
But he never saw his friends again.

Now he can't get it off,
It's stuck to his skin.
The mask is taking over,
It's controlling him.

His left hand doesn't know
What his right hand is doing.
His arms and legs can't tell
If they're coming or going.
His head feels as if
It's on back to front.
He can't say or do
A single thing he wants.

Stuck on his face!
Stuck on his face!
He's got a mask
Stuck on his face!
He's not who he was,
An extraordinary case.
He's got a mask
Stuck on his face!

Head In A Box

When you've had enough of yourself
Put your head in a box.
Unless you are a young child
You'll find a shoebox is too small.
If you have a wooden chest with a padlock
So much the better.
If you cannot find a suitable receptacle
You will have to make your own container.
Take care. In the state you're in
You might hit your hand with a hammer.

When you have everything prepared
Grip your head firmly.

Do not pull the ears, tug the hair,
Poke the eyes or tweak the nose.
This will only make matters worse
And could be considered by some
To constitute bullying.
After all,
You are tormenting yourself too much already.

Watch out! Your head might bite you.
If it does, try not to drop it
As this could damage it beyond repair.
If it struggles and slips out of your fingers
It will endeavour to escape
By bouncing or rolling away.
This should be avoided at all costs.
Make sure all doors and windows are closed
Before attempting this procedure.

Place your head securely in the box.
Do not wait beside it
As you may find its behaviour disturbing
And its cries distressing.
It might even start saying the sort of things
You want to hear.
Don't be deceived.

Remember, you are the one in control.
You decide when your head will be let out
of the box.

Get out of earshot.
Go for a walk.
Have a cup of tea.
Take a holiday – a proper holiday.

No, seriously,
Whatever you do,
You must leave your head for at least an hour,
A day or two if possible,
A month, ideally.

When you return to the box
Do not take your head by surprise.
Gently knock three times
And slowly lift the lid to accustom
The eyes to the light.
Don't say anything
But calmly put it back where it was
When this all started.

Keep the box in a place that is easy to access.
Repeat this procedure as many times as necessary.

Let's Go For A Walk, Dear!

I play football,
I go swimming,
I love table tennis too.

I like hockey,
I love surfing,
There are so many sports to do.
I'm so active,
Seldom static,
And I always try my best, but sometimes
I get so exhausted,
That's when I sit down to rest.

But then my mum appears,
With a grin from ear to ear.
I know that I should fear,
The next words I will hear.

'Let's go for a walk, dear!'
Oh no!
'Let's go for a walk, dear!'
Oh no!

'Come on, let's get some fresh air,
You need more exercise.
It's not good slumping in your chair
And lounging around inside.
You'll feel much better for it,
It will help you lose some weight.

Get up! Look smart! Shape up! Go!
I'll race you to the gate.'

When I hear those words,
I want to run a mile, but not
Over hills or through the woods
And jumping over stiles.
I'd do anything to stay indoors,
Anything at all.
I'd even do my brother's chores,
It drives me up the wall!

'Let's go for a walk, dear!'
Oh no!
'Let's go for a walk, dear!'
Oh no!

'Come on dear, here's your waterproofs,
Please don't be a pain.
It's probably best to wear your boots,
It looks like it might rain.
Hat and gloves are in the drawer,
No, I'm not your slave.
What on earth are your legs for?
Come on, please, behave!'

I'll do the washing up,
I'll tidy up my room.
I'll do it now, I promise
And I don't mean soon.
I won't steal your make-up,
I'll never ever moan.
I'm prepared to compromise,
Just let me stay at home.

'Let's go for a walk, dear!'
Oh no!
'Let's go for a walk, dear!'
Oh no!

'Come on, dear, please be more tough
You won't get that sleepover
And the sooner we set off,
The sooner it's all over.
And when we both get back,
We'll quickly have our tea.
And then you can relax
And have a game of golf with me!'

Sasha Squished A Spider

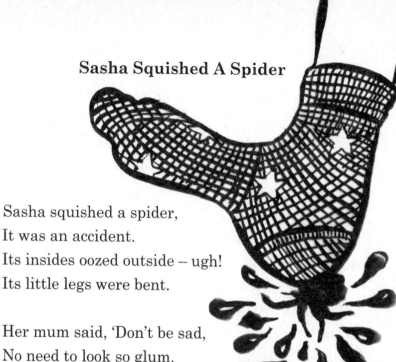

Sasha squished a spider,
It was an accident.
Its insides oozed outside – ugh!
Its little legs were bent.

Her mum said, 'Don't be sad,
No need to look so glum.
Some good can come from bad,
Let's make another one.

'Take this tasty meatball,
Add eight thin frozen chips.
Choc-chips make great eyeballs,
Or even orange pips.'

Then it clambered to the rafters
Like a Himalayan yeti,
And lived happily ever after
In a web made of spaghetti.

Old Spider And The Giant Clam Shell

Creation Story from Micronesia.

No sun – no moon – no land – just ocean and – nothing – and then – from above – Old Spider comes down – and there – on the ocean – drifts a Giant Clam Shell.

Old Spider taps – Old Spider knocks – a hollow sound – an empty sound.

Old Spider chants – Old Spider sings – the Giant Clam Shell opens – Old Spider slips in.

Dark as pitch – black as coal – inside – too cramped to stretch – she crawls – she reaches out and touches something round and smooth – a coil-like form – then wet and soft – a snail – a snail?

She takes the snail and places it beneath her so that her magic might work upon it – and then she sleeps – and when she wakes she sets it free to wend its slimy way.

But dark as pitch – black as coal – inside – too cramped to stretch – she crawls – she reaches out and touches something round and smooth – a coil-like form – wet and soft – a snail? – a second snail – larger than the first – she places it beneath her and then reaches for the smaller snail and asks – 'Can you open this shell a little – so that I can sit?'

And it was done.

The halves of the Giant Clam Shell parted and Old Spider stretched her legs at last – but dark – it was still so dark – Old Spider took the first snail and put it in the west – in the upper half of the shell and this became – the moon.

Now there was a silvery light to see by – and by this light Old Spider saw a large worm in the bottom of the shell and asked – 'Can you open this shell a little – so that I can stand?'

The worm said 'Yes,' and began to push – to stretch and strain – to heave and ho – *creaks and groans* – until the halves of the Giant Clam Shell were prised wide open.

So much sweat the worm had oozed – warm and wet – it lay in the lower shell and this became the salty sea.

But the worm's work was not yet done – it wrenched the Giant Clam Shell in two and raised the upper half high above – and this became – the sky.

And then the worm lay down to die – breaking into many pieces – and these became – the islands.

And then Old Spider took the second snail and placed it in the east of the sky – and it became – the sun – our sun that lights the day.

And this is how Old Spider made our world – from a Giant Clam Shell – many, many years ago.

Seaweed Seahorse

I found a little seahorse
On the shingle shore,
Lying on some seaweed
Whilst the waves did roar.

When from a nearby rock pool
Came a scuttling crab
Set on snaffling its next meal,
I quickly made a grab.

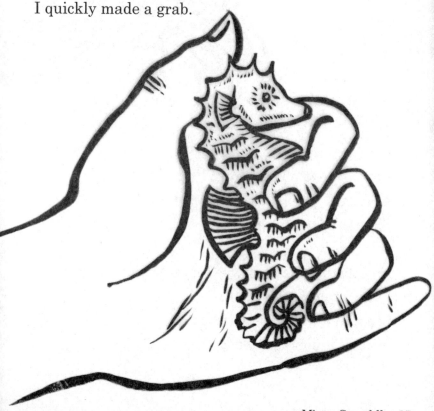

It nipped my little finger
And I yelped out in pain,
A seagull swooped and scooped it off
Then it began to rain.

And though the seahorse seemed asleep
I knew that it was dead,
I couldn't bear to leave it there
So took it home instead.

Sofia And The Sea Of Tears

There was once a princess who lived in an apricot palace in the middle of a desert. Every morning she looked from her window and saw hot air shimmering over rolling sand dunes. She imagined them rising and falling beneath the orange sun like the waves of an ocean.

At breakfast her brother flicked date stones at her and laughed,

'Sofia is daydreaming about the sea again!'

'Don't listen to him,' their mother said, 'Hassam has lost his imagination and is jealous.'

Sofia smiled sadly at the prince and kicked off her sandals.

As she walked barefoot into the desert, the sand trickled between her toes. Out of the heat haze appeared a traveller on a camel who passed by and disappeared. A lizard darted under a rock. Suddenly she felt very lonely.

When she was a little girl, her grandfather told her stories of sailors who sailed the seven seas and of winds that whipped the water into waves that could wash away a million sand dunes. She heard of caves where monsters lurked and coves where mermaids

sat on rocks combing seaweed from their glistening hair.

Sofia wanted to know what sea water tasted like. She wondered how long she could hold her breath, how deep could she dive and how many little fish can a big fish eat in a day? She wanted to float on her back and to stare at the sky and be carried away by wave after wave after wave to an unknown island out in a mysterious ocean.

The princess dawdled in the desert, lost in seadreams beneath an azure sky when, out of the blue, a hot blast of air took her breath away and she was swept up in a sandstorm and then dumped like a coconut on the ridge of a deserted dune.

Salt water sprayed from her eyes and fell to the ground like rain. A stream became a river flowing into the Sea of Tears.

Waves licked the toes of the desert princess sitting on the shore.

Mermaids frolicked with seahorses and whales played ball with seals.

A sailor with a stripey top was rapidly rowing a tiny boat from a sinking ship. A ten-tongued sea beast rose from the depths with a whiplash roar. Sofia held her breath, dived into the sea and shot like a shark towards the monster. She pulled a face and it fled in terror.

Sofia slipped into the rowing boat and said, 'Sixty-seven seconds.'

'What?' said the sailor, whose name was Sinbad.

'That's how long I can hold my breath for,' she replied.

'Oh,' said Sinbad, 'and where did you come from?'

She pointed across the water. There beside the sea was an apricot palace beneath an orange sun. Waving on the beach were her mother, Hassam and her grandfather.

'What does the sea taste like?' her brother asked later that evening.

'Tears,' laughed Sofia and Sinbad together. 'It tastes of tears.'

Ship In The Bottle

When Grandad died
he was toasting bread on the electric fire,
and when his heart stopped
the cork popped out of the bottle on the mantelpiece
and sea spurted into the living room.

The ship's horn boomed
and a Toby jug toppled from the shelf
and sank bubbling to the carpet.

Grandad was bobbing up and down
drifting towards the window,
but a seagull's cry
woke the tattooed mermaid on his chest.

She slipped from his skin
and swam with him into the bottle
and laid him gently on the bridge.

And when she kissed him,
his eyes opened
and he stood and took the helm.

A whistle blew, the engine started.
He raised the inky anchor
on his forearm,
waved farewell
and sailed across the seven seas.

And when I take the cork out of the bottle
I smell the steamer's smoke,
I taste the tang of sea,
I hear the seagull's cries
and know the ship
that Grandad made
will one day come for me.

The Wicked Pumpkin

In a town you've never heard of, in a street you'll never walk down and in a house you'll never see, lived a little boy called Eustace. He was exceptionally good most of the time, but occasionally was very bad indeed. His mother and father didn't like it when he misbehaved and had warned him that if he did anything naughty ever again he'd wish he'd never been born.

Early every Monday morning, before Eustace was awake, his father would set off to work in a faraway town where he'd stay until the end of the week. After breakfast, Eustace walked five miles to school and his mother would spend the day at Lazy Zak's, coming back just in time for supper which Eustace had to have on the table by six o'clock sharp.

After clearing the kitchen table he'd go to his room in the damp, cold cellar while his mother sat at the kitchen table playing patience. When his father returned on Friday evening Eustace would be asked if he'd been a good boy in his absence.

Now, one Saturday afternoon in spring, while his father was watching football on the TV and his mother was nowhere to be seen, Eustace was putting the lawn mower away in the garden shed when a mouse shot between his feet and disappeared between two tins of creosote. Eustace rushed over to see if the little creature might have a nest hidden in a cosy corner.

 Behind a stack of fallen flower pots there was a dusty wooden box. He thought

it was probably full of old tools he'd neither know the name of, nor what to do with, but when he nudged it with his foot it was lighter than expected and, in the wall behind, he noticed a tiny hole through which the mouse must have escaped. He took the box to the daylight and crouched in the doorway with it on his lap. Puffing a cloud of woodworm dust into the air, he wiped away the cobwebs with his sleeve and drew out out the metal pin of the catch. The rusty hinges creaked as he opened the lid.

There was nothing inside but a couple of dead beetles and what looked like a woodchip. When he held it in his palm, he could see it was actually a seed, oval and shrivelled like a sweet that had been sucked dry and then spat out. Disappointed with his find, he flicked the seed into the garden, threw the box on to the woodpile and spent the rest of the afternoon perched in a pear tree on the railway embankment.

Above the house that night, a thunderstorm shot darts of rain from dark and angry clouds. Lightning flashes filled the sky and one bolt scorched the earth and struck the seed, waking it from its slumber. Jolted to life and lashed by rain, the seed was pummelled into the soil and there it lay catching its breath before flicking forth the tiny tongue of a shoot to worm its way through the sodden tilth.

Roots like hairy tentacles clawed into the earth and before the week had passed, two tiny green leaves sprang forth blinking in the morning light. And even though the spring frosts were not yet over, the keenest morning snap did not stall or kill that little seedling.

Soon, great umbrellas of leaves rose from the ground and on the first day of June, a single yellow trumpet flower bloomed triumphantly before wilting and withering away. The beginnings of a queer vegetable protruded from the plant – a green and white speckled knob shaped like an amputee's stump which by the summer holidays had grown into the shape of a large football. By the first chill days of autumn, a great orange pumpkin, the size of a cow's head, was lying snugly upon a bed of straw.

That the seed had germinated had been a pleasant surprise to Eustace and he had lovingly nurtured it since he had noticed its presence in the spring. Indeed, he spent many a happy hour tending to the growing plant's needs and had begun to think of the pumpkin as his one and only friend, confiding in it his secrets and his fears.

But, even though to anyone but you or me it might have seemed a completely ordinary kind of pumpkin, it wasn't really, it was only pretending – biding its time. Eustace had yet to find out that what was growing in his little patch by the garden shed was really a most Wicked Pumpkin.

Now, one Monday morning in the last week of October, Eustace was on his way to school when he did something that was very naughty, but since no-one had seen him do it, it was his own little secret.

But when he came home from school and walked down the garden path, he heard the Wicked Pumpkin say,

'I know what you did on the way to school today and I'm going to tell your parents.'

'Oh, please don't tell them,' begged Eustace, 'I'll do anything you ask me to.'

'All right,' said the Wicked Pumpkin, 'I won't tell them if you sprinkle salt on the soil to stop the slugs and snails eating my leaves. I want to watch them squirm and ooze white bubbles as they die a horrible death.'

Well, is that what Eustace did? Yes, that's just what Eustace did.

Now, on the Tuesday morning in the last week of October, Eustace was in the playground when he did something which was very, very naughty, but since no-one had seen him do it, it was his own little secret.

But when he came home from school and walked down the garden path, he heard the Wicked Pumpkin say,

'I know what you did in the playground today and I'm going to tell your parents.'

'Oh, please don't tell them,' pleaded Eustace, 'I'll do anything you ask me to.'

'All right,' said the Wicked Pumpkin, 'I won't tell them if you steal your mother's golden necklace and hang it around my neck so I look pretty.'

Well, is that what Eustace did? Yes, that's just what Eustace did.

Now, on the Wednesday morning in the last week of October, Eustace was in the classroom when he did something which was very, very, very naughty, but since no-one had seen him do it, it was his own little secret.

But when he came home from school and walked down the garden path, he heard the Wicked Pumpkin say,

'I know what you did in the classroom today and I'm going to tell your parents.'

'Oh, please don't tell them,' implored Eustace, 'I'll do anything you ask me to'.

'All right,' said the Wicked Pumpkin, 'I won't tell them if you shoot all of the birds in the garden with your air pistol. They wake me up every morning with their silly songs.'

Well, is that what Eustace did? Yes, that's just what Eustace did.

Now, on the Thursday lunchtime in the last week of October,

Eustace was in the school canteen when he did something which was very, very, very, very naughty, but since no-one had seen him do it, it was his own little secret.

But when he came home from school and walked down the garden path, he heard the Wicked Pumpkin say,

'I know what you did in the dining hall today and I'm going to tell your parents.'

'Oh, please don't tell them,' appealed Eustace, 'I'll do anything you ask me to.'

'All right,' said the Wicked Pumpkin, 'I won't tell them if you bash that croaky toad that lives in the flower pot with a brick.'

Well, is that what Eustace did? Yes, that's just what Eustace did.

Now, on the Friday afternoon in the last week of October, as he was walking home, Eustace watched the fire engines racing to his school.

He had done something very, very, very, very, very naughty, but since no-one had seen him do it, it was his own little secret.

But when he came home from school and walked down the garden path, he heard the Wicked Pumpkin say,

'I know what you did at school today and I'm going to tell your parents.'

'Oh, please don't tell them,' entreated Eustace, 'I'll do anything you ask me to.'

'All right,' said the Wicked Pumpkin, 'I won't tell them if you take that axe and chop off the head of next door's cat. She keeps coming into our garden to use it as a toilet.'

Well, is that what Eustace did? No, that's *not* what Eustace did.

Our Eustace picked up the axe and chopped

off the Wicked Pumpkin's head. He was about to cleave it clean in half when the Wicked Pumpkin rolled along the garden path and out through the garden gate. Eustace ran into the street but it was nowhere to be seen.

'At last,' thought Eustace, 'my secrets are safe.'

And in he went to make the supper.

At six o'clock that evening, his mother and he were sat at the table when his father came home from work carrying a big orange pumpkin. He put it in the middle of the table and said,

'Look what I found by the garden gate. Someone has left us a treat for tomorrow evening's celebrations. After supper we'll hollow it out and carve a face and put a candle inside. But first things first, Eustace, have you been a good boy this week?'

'Oh yes,' he replied, 'I've been a very good boy.'

But then the Wicked Pumpkin said,

'Oh no you haven't, you've been a very bad boy.'

And it told the parents all the naughty things Eustace had done.

Eustace was very ashamed and said he was very, very, very, very, very sorry and wouldn't do any of those things again.

His father stood up and told him to go to his room. While he was walking down the stairs to the cellar he heard his mother and father both exclaim,

'Goodness knows, what are we going to do with that boy?'

They were up half the night discussing the

possibilities but it wasn't until the Wicked Pumpkin offered a suggestion that they made a decision.

If the Trick-or-Treaters who trooped down the garden path the next evening had looked closer at the gruesome head glowing on the porch, they might have noticed that it wasn't really a small carved pumpkin after all. Then perhaps, they wouldn't have waited so keenly for Eustace's parents to open the door.

Terrible Trolls

Trolls, trolls – terrible trolls!
Trolls, trolls – wonderful trolls!
Trolls, trolls – abominable trolls!
Trolls, trolls – unbelievable trolls!

Trolls, we are so horrible
We make our own flesh creep.
We roam about at nightfall
As people go to sleep.

We burst into your bedrooms
And drag you to our caves.
We then demand a ransom
From your weeping relatives.

Trolls, trolls – terrible trolls!
If you want to survive you must pay a toll.
Trolls, trolls – terrible trolls!
Else we'll eat you alive, yes, we're in control.

We love hoards of treasure
As much as we can steal.
It gives us as much pleasure
As listening to you squeal.

We have to fight with heroes
Who try to rescue you.
But they are really zeroes
We bung them in the stew.

Trolls, trolls – terrible trolls!
We are so cool, we are so droll.
Trolls, trolls – terrible trolls!
We are not cute pretty little dolls.

Terrorising is such fun
We'd do it all the time
But we're restricted by the sun
It hurts us when it shines.

We love to make you jump with fright
But one thing makes us groan.
If we're out 'til morning light
Then we turn to stone.

Trolls, trolls – terrible trolls!
If you want to survive you must pay a toll.
Trolls, trolls – terrible trolls!
Else we'll eat you alive, yes, we're in control.

Trolls, trolls – terrible trolls!
We are so cool, we are so droll.
Trolls, trolls – terrible trolls!
We are not cute pretty little dolls.

Suzanne Loved A Snowman

Suzanne
loved a snowman

they liked to
kiss and cuddle

but then
her heart was broken

he left her
in a puddle.

Robin Distressed

While I dug the veggie patch
you'd dart between my legs
and snaffle lovely larvae,
wriggly worms and sweet snail eggs.

When I'd poured a mug of tea
from my thermos flask,
I'd flick you bread or biscuit crumbs,
I'd give you anything you asked.

You'd perch upon the handle
of my garden fork.
We'd whistle tunes in unison
then have a little talk.

That spring was like our honeymoon
but then you went all fussy.
You turned up your beak at bugs and slugs,
you became quite huffy.

You'd only peck the choicest fare
from a china plate.

No longer would you tolerate cake
past its sell-by date.

And now the snow lies all around
the ground is hard with frost.
You look distressed in your little red vest
but you can just get lost.

It's no good making eyes at me
from the bare bird table.
This tale I'll tell to my grandchild,
he likes to hear a fable.

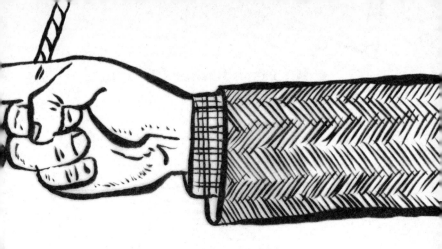

For now that it is Christmas Day
I have no Brussels sprouts.
I don't have the home-grown veg I want,
I have to go without.

Caterpillars you declined,
dined on my brassicas all summer.
So now it's winter you will starve,
you fussy little duffer.

No, I'll not feed you nuts or seeds
– for you're no friend of mine.
Tweet your last breath then freeze to death
– your feet stuck to the washing line.

A Gift From Father Christmas

Old Father Christmas
Has the flu.
No 'HO HO HOs!'
But just, 'Atchoooooooo!'

With dripping nose
And aching head,
He hauls his moped
From the shed.

He coughs and splutters
To the school
And doles out presents
In the hall.

The pupils, staff
And PTA,
Lie ill in bed
Come Christmas Day.

Short Song

There
are
very
few
words
in this
song

that's
why it
doesn't
last
very
long.

Short Story

Once upon a time,

happened...

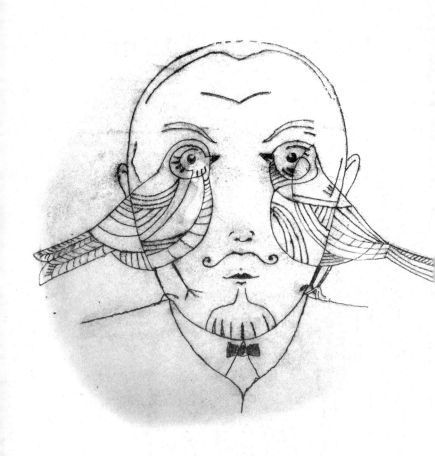